THERE IS MY PEOPLE SLEEPING

A TRULY BEAUTIFUL BOOK

FOR A TRULY BEAUTIFUL PERSON

OUEN

SNOWBIRD

The Ethnic
Poem-Drawings of

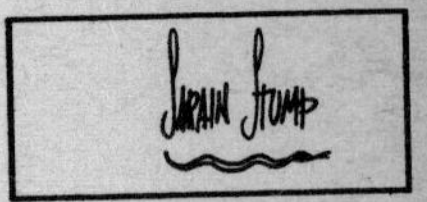

GRAY'S PUBLISHING LTD.
SIDNEY
BRITISH COLUMBIA
CANADA

THERE IS MY PEOPLE SLEEPING

THIS BOOK I DEDICATE TO
Mrs. GEORGE CHATTAWAY
OF THE *BAR-S* RANCH
WHO HAS ALWAYS BEEN INTERESTED
IN THE ART AND WELFARE
OF MY PEOPLE

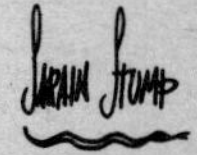

THERE IS MY PEOPLE SLEEPING

LIKE LITTLE HANDS
   THE FLOWERS
BREAK FROM THE GROUND
   TO STEAL
LITTLE DROPS OF SUN

LIKE LITTLE HANDS

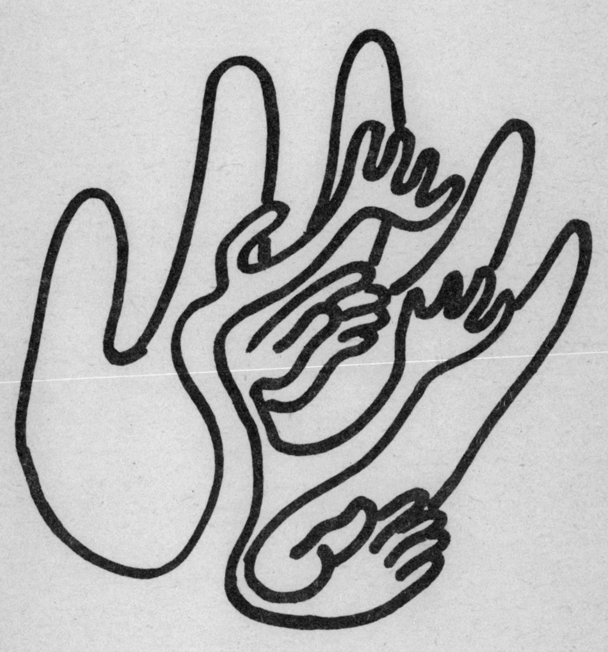

THE FLOWERS
BREAK FROM THE GROUND

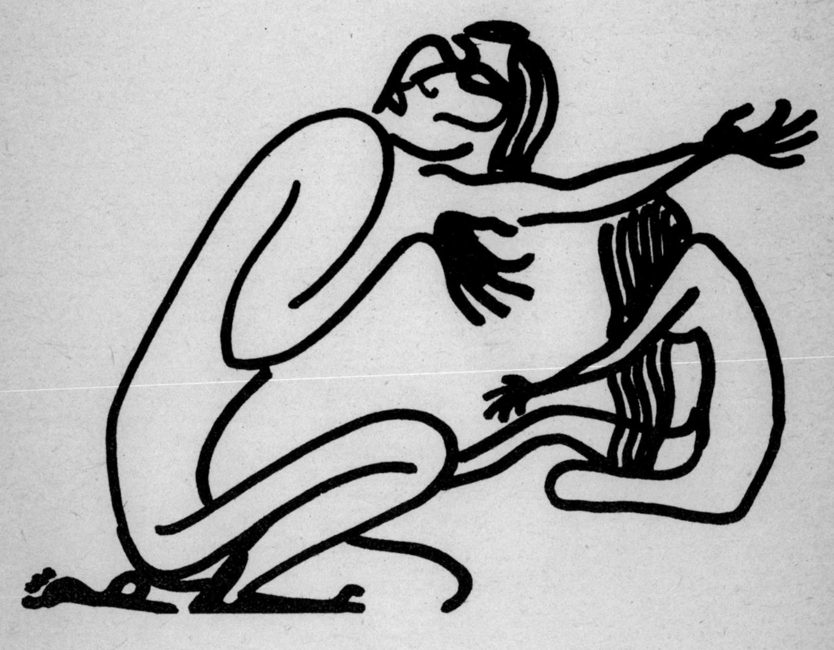

TO STEAL

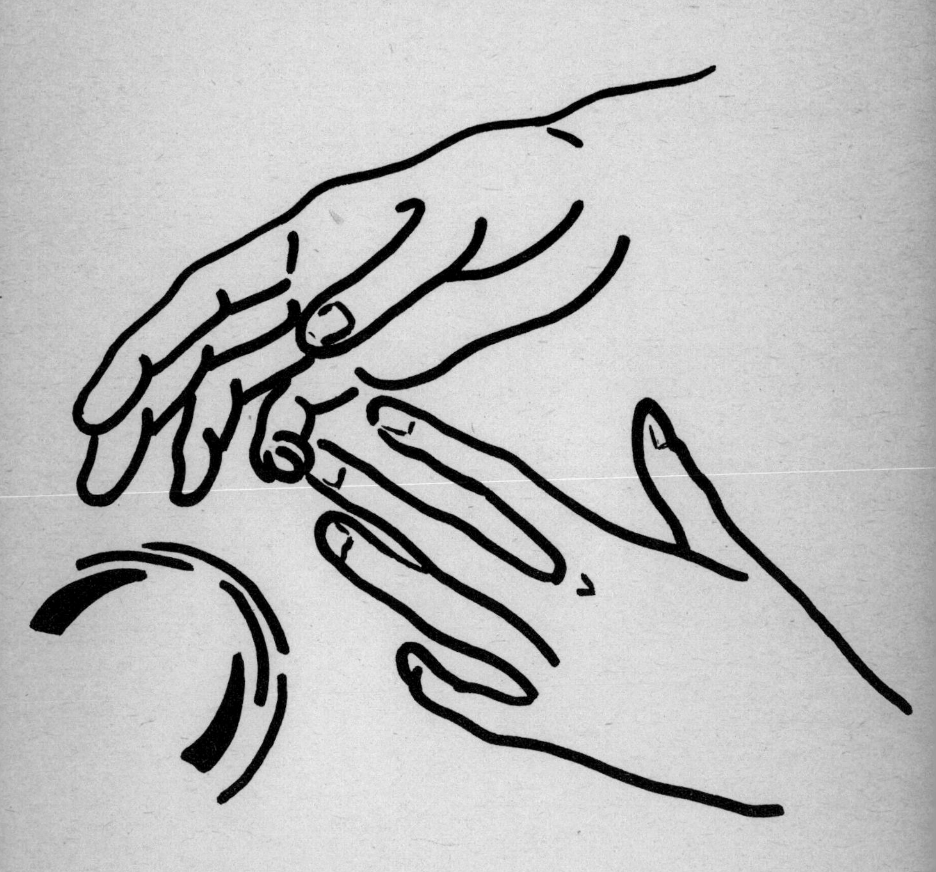

LITTLE DROPS OF SUN

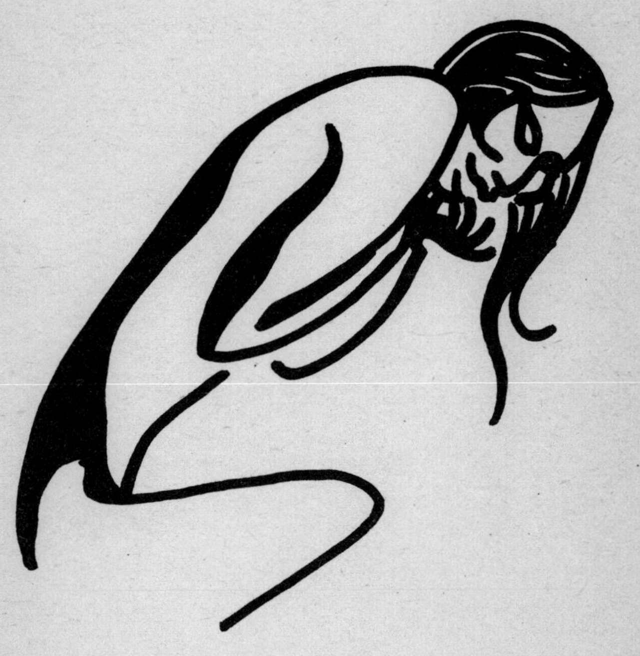

AND THERE IS MY PEOPLE SLEEPING
SINCE A LONG TIME
BUT AREN'T JUST DREAMS
THE OLD CARS WITHOUT ENGINE
PARKING IN FRONT OF THE HOUSE
OR ANGRY WORDS ORDERING PEACE OF MIND
OR WHO STEALS FROM YOU FOR YOUR GOOD
AND DOESN'T WANNA REMEMBER WHAT HE OWES YOU
SOMETIMES I'D LIKE TO FALL ASLEEP TOO,
CLOSE MY EYES ON EVERYTHING

   BUT I CAN'T
      I CAN'T

AND THERE IS MY PEOPLE SLEEPING

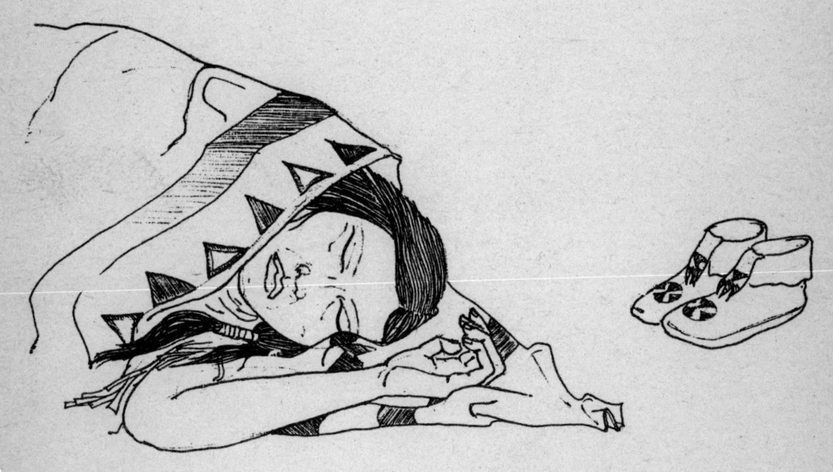

SINCE A LONG TIME

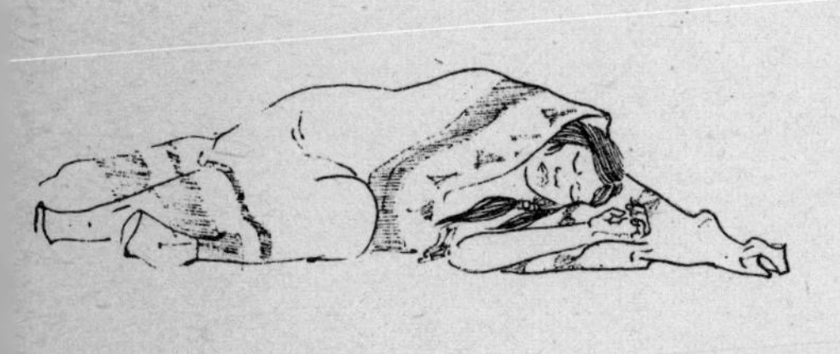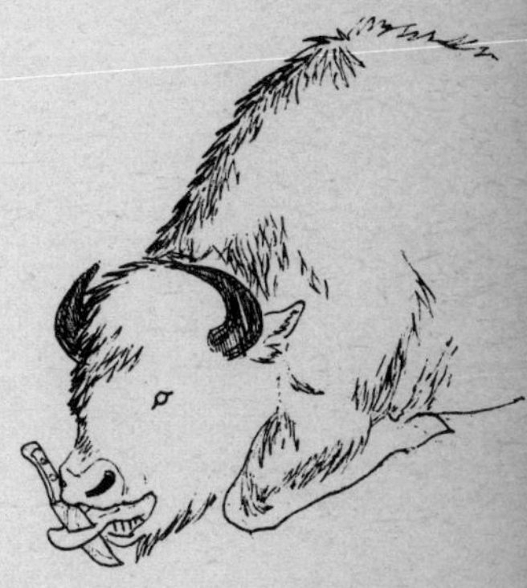

BUT AREN'T JUST DREAMS
THE OLD CARS WITHOUT ENGINE
PARKING IN FRONT OF THE HOUSE

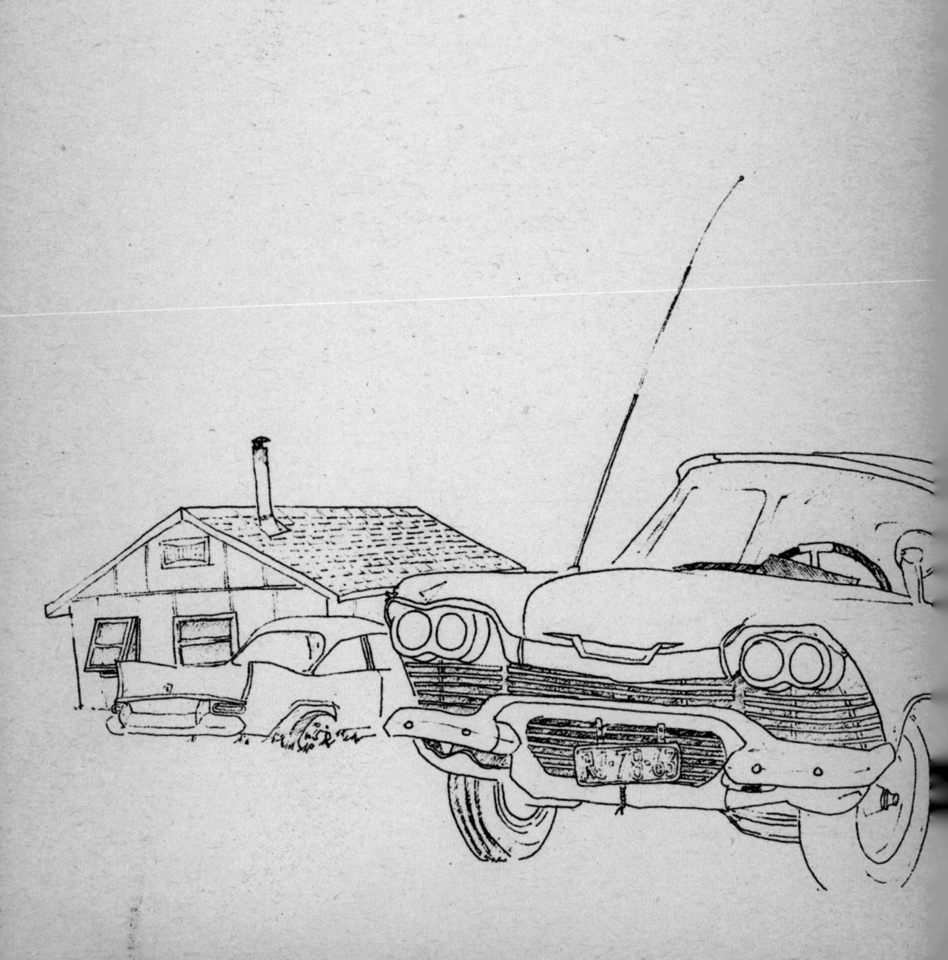

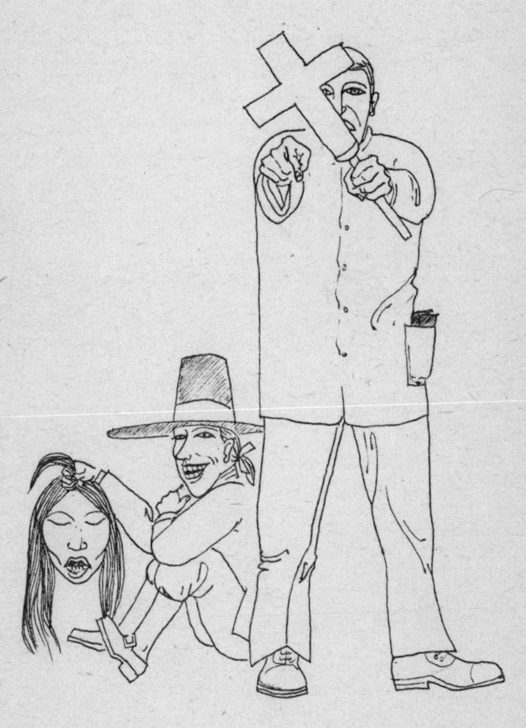

OR WHO STEALS FROM YOU FOR YOUR GOOD

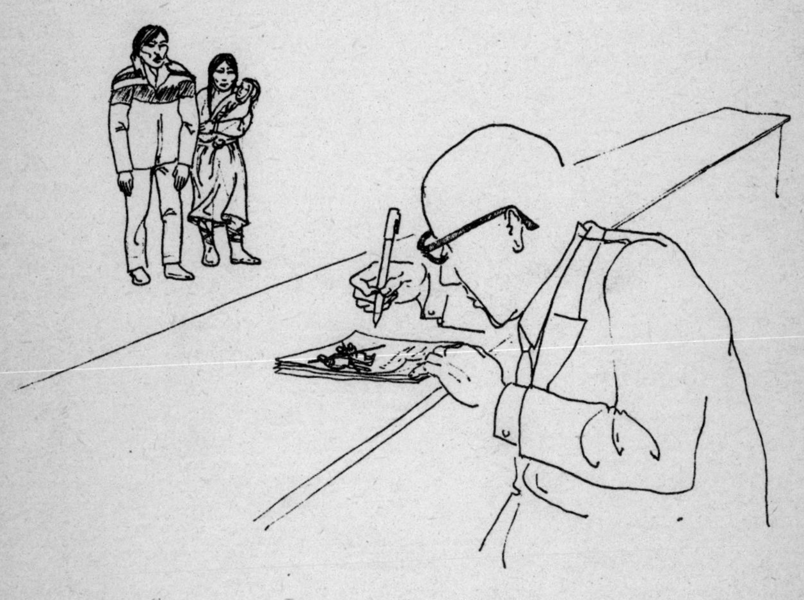

AND DOESN'T WANNA REMEMBER WHAT HE OWES YOU

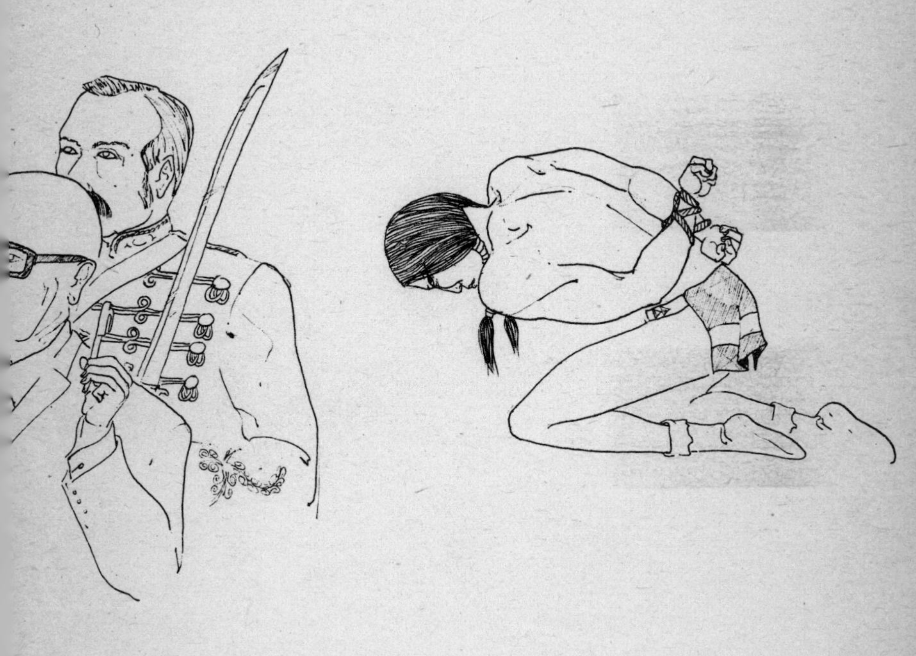

SOMETIMES I'D LIKE TO FALL ASLEEP TOO,
CLOSE MY EYES ON EVERYTHING

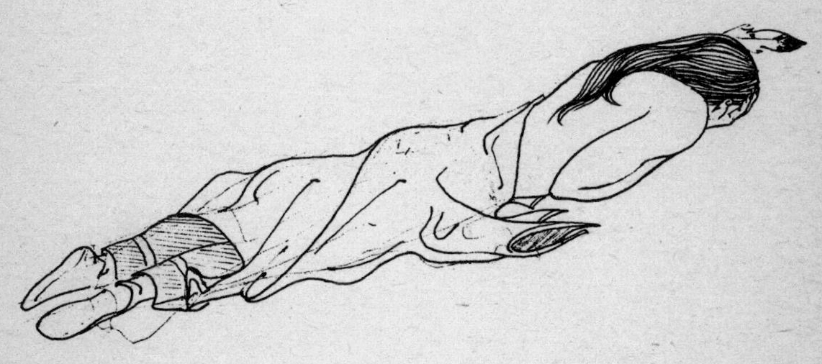

BUT I CAN'T

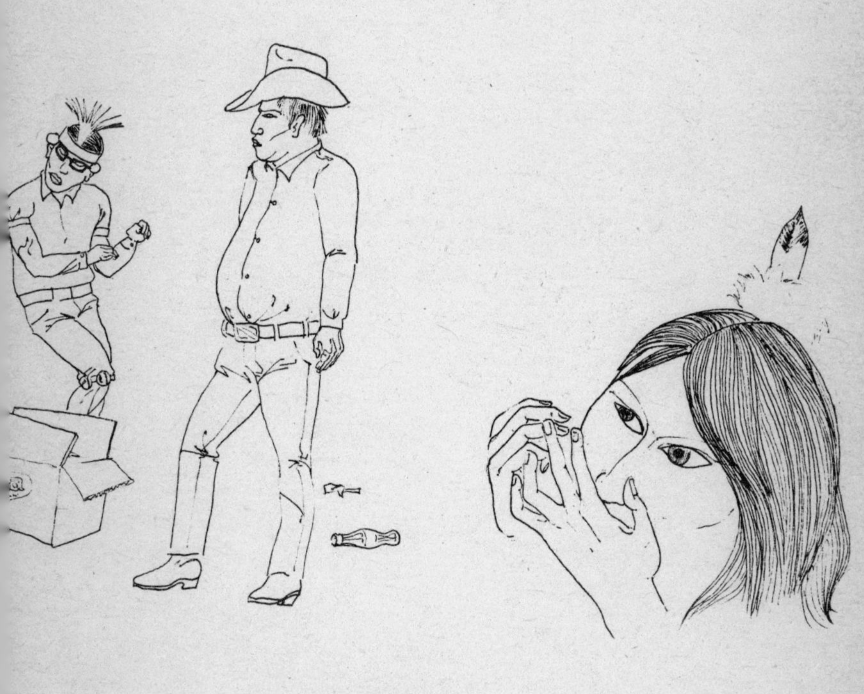

I CAN'T

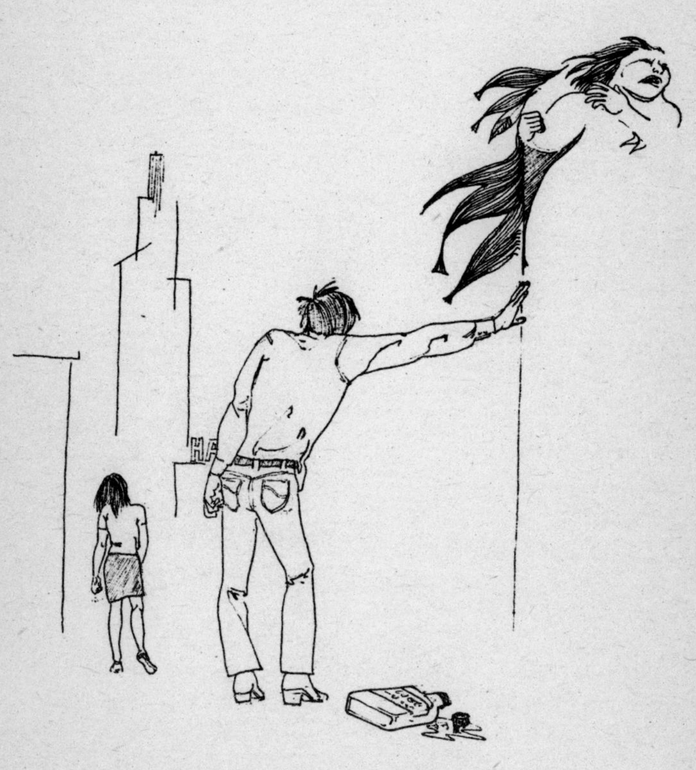

IT'S WITH TERROR, SOMETIMES
THAT I HEAR THEM CALLING ME
BUT IT'S THE LIGHT SKIP OF A COUGAR
DETACHING ME FROM THE GROUND
TO LEAVE ME ALONE
WITH MY CRAZY POWER
TILL I REACH THE SUN MAKERS
AND FIND MYSELF AGAIN
IN A NEW PLACE

IT'S WITH TERROR, SOMETIMES
THAT I HEAR THEM CALLING ME

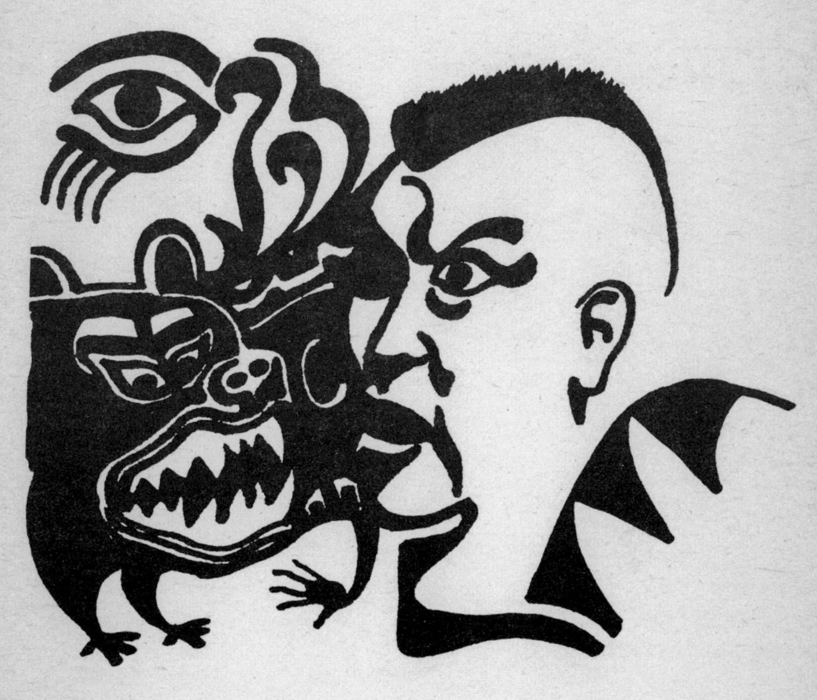

BUT IT'S THE LIGHT SKIP OF A COUGAR
DETACHING ME FROM THE GROUND

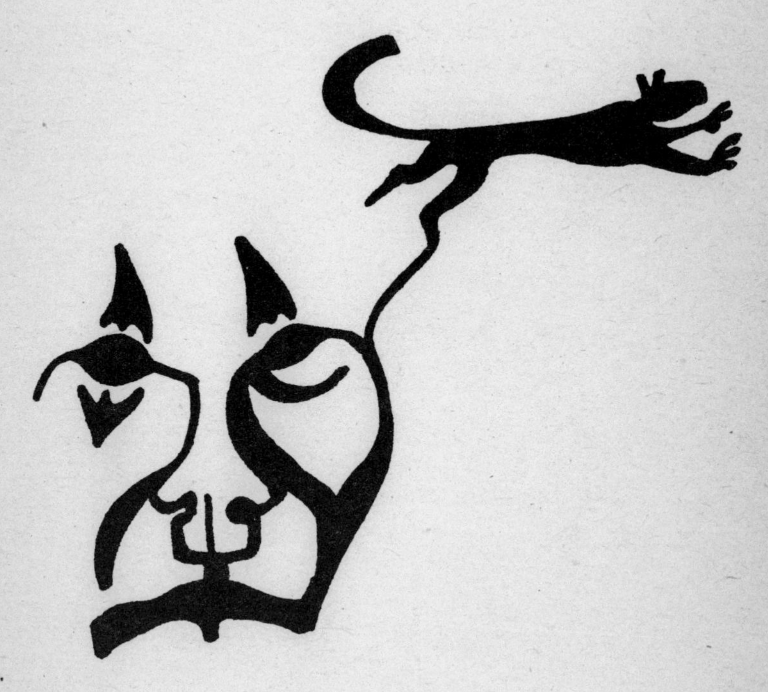

TO LEAVE ME ALONE
WITH MY CRAZY POWER

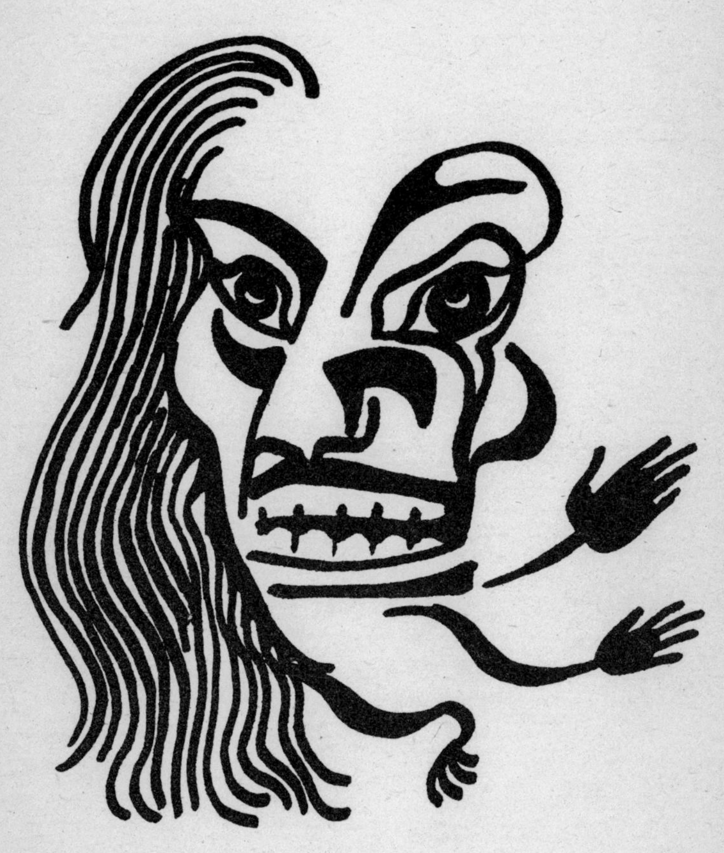

TILL I REACH THE SUN MAKERS

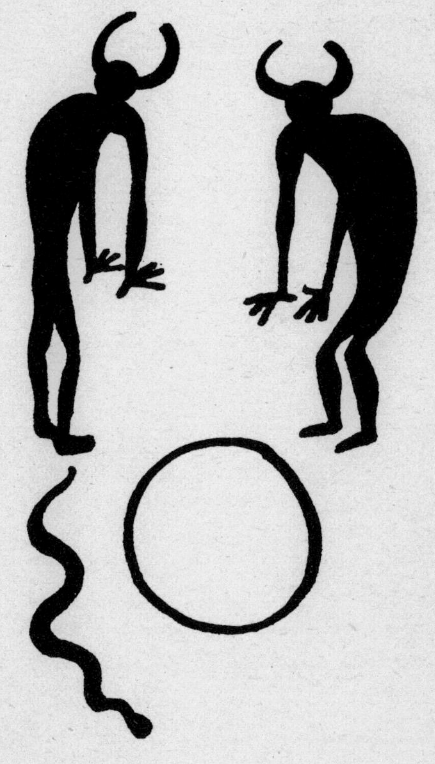

AND FIND MYSELF AGAIN
IN A NEW PLACE

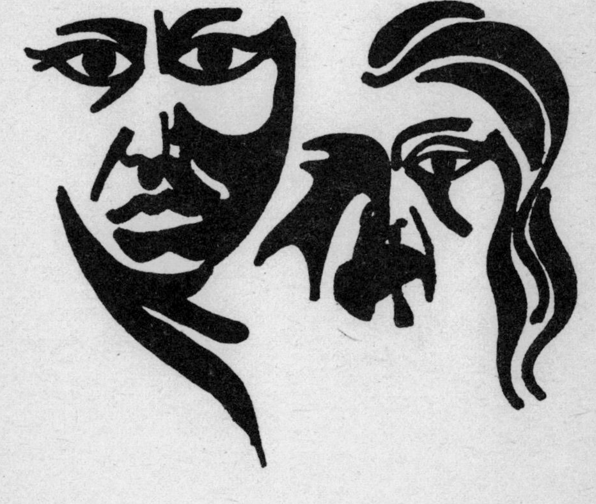

HE GOES AWAY
VERY FAR AWAY
WITHOUT ANYBODY ON HIS TAIL
TEETH OF SNAKE, BIRD'S WINGS
THE SHAMAN GOES FAR AWAY

HE GOES AWAY

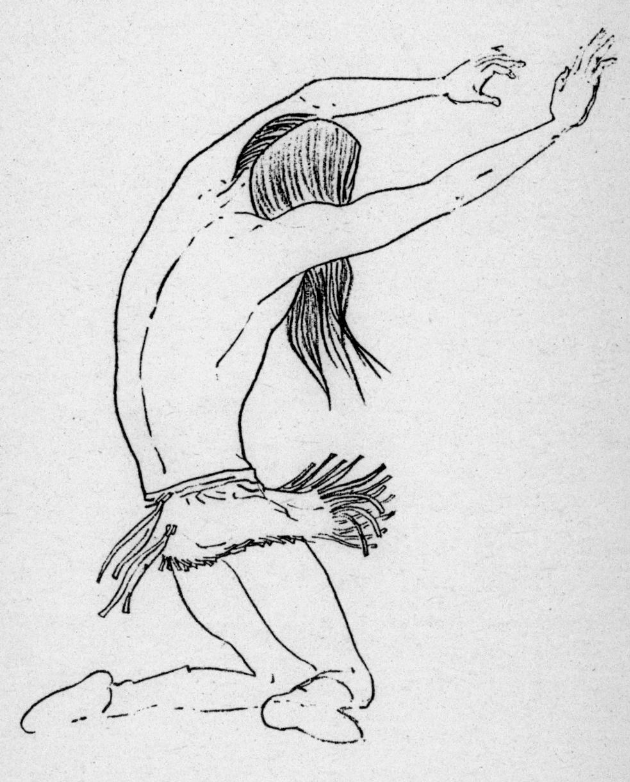

VERY FAR AWAY

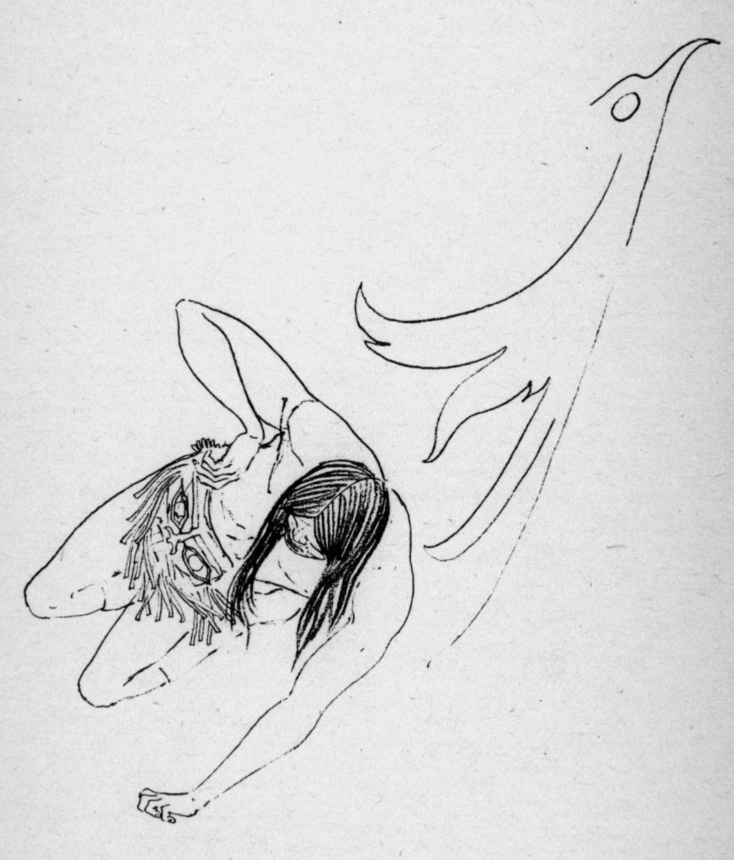

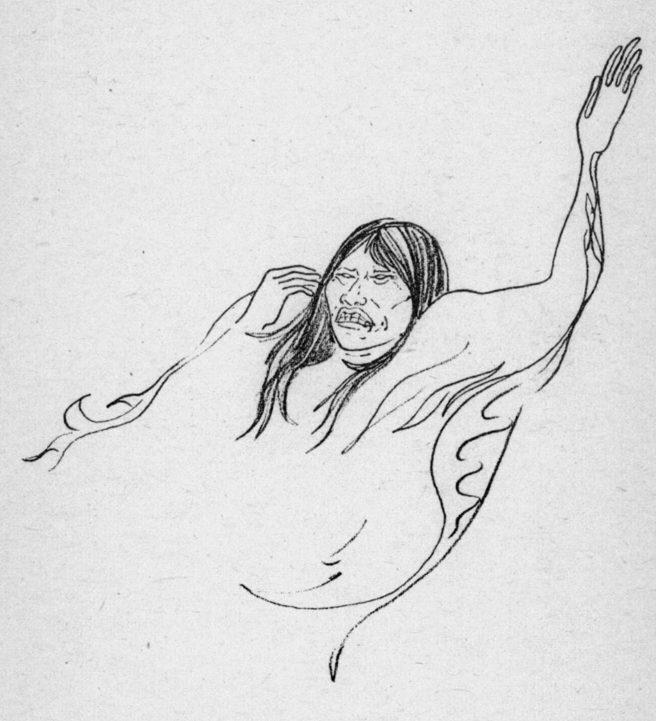

TEETH OF SNAKE, BIRD'S WINGS

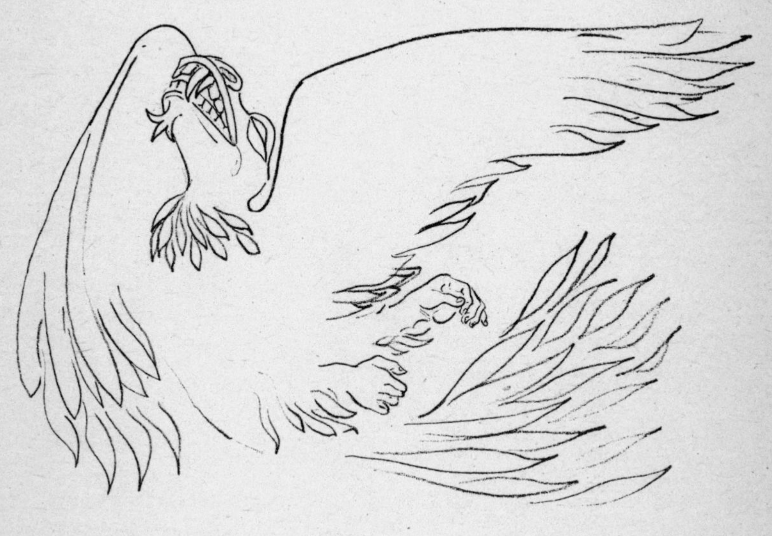

THE SHAMAN GOES FAR AWAY

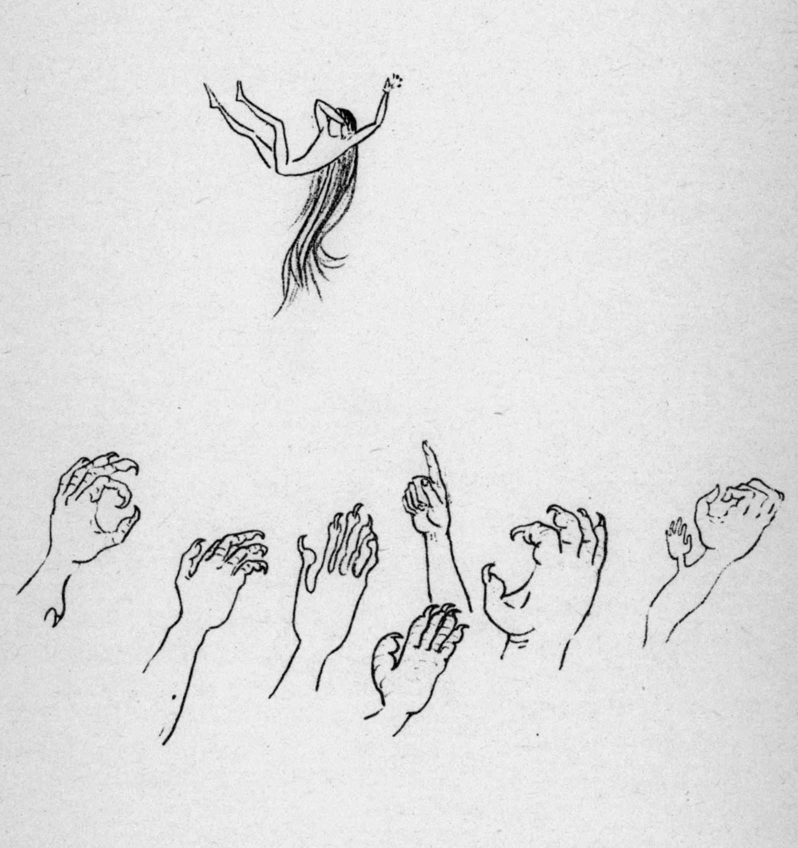

GOTTA BE THE BEST
AT THE BALL GAME
AND HUNT SOMETHING
EVERYTIME I GO FOR A WALK
PUT TOGETHER A FEW WISE WORDS
IN FRONT OF THE ELDER ONES
ALL BECAUSE SHE SMILED AT ME
AND HER FATHER SAID
HE AIN'T GONNA GIVE HER
TO WHO'S NOT A MAN

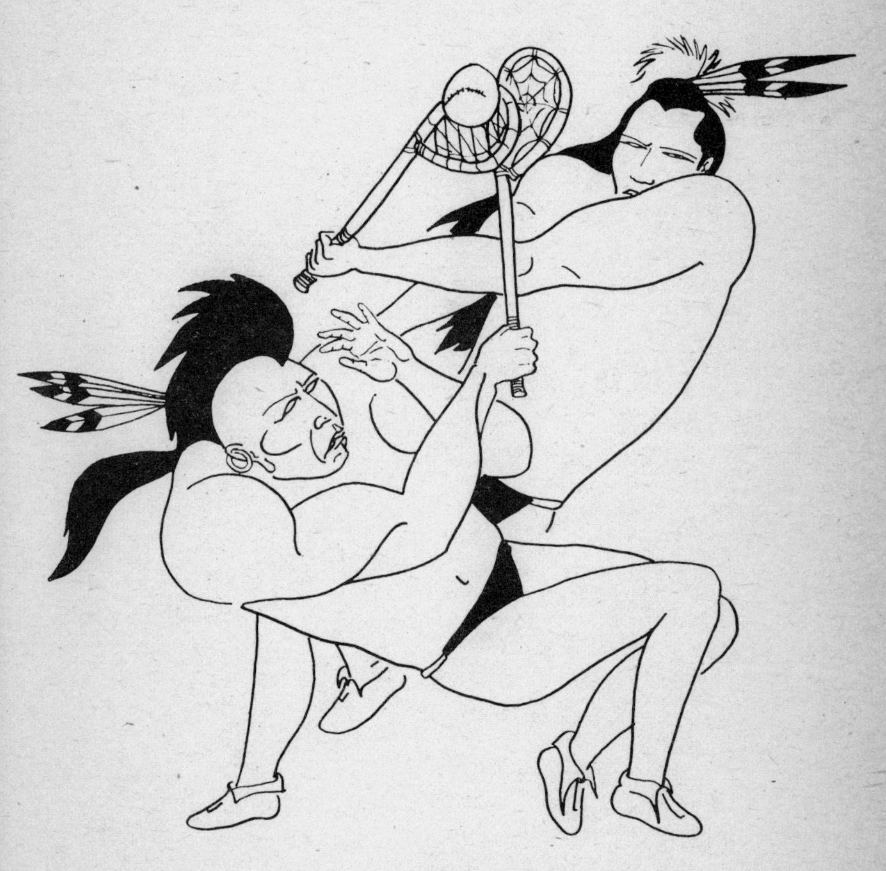

AND HUNT SOMETHING
EVERYTIME I GO FOR A WALK

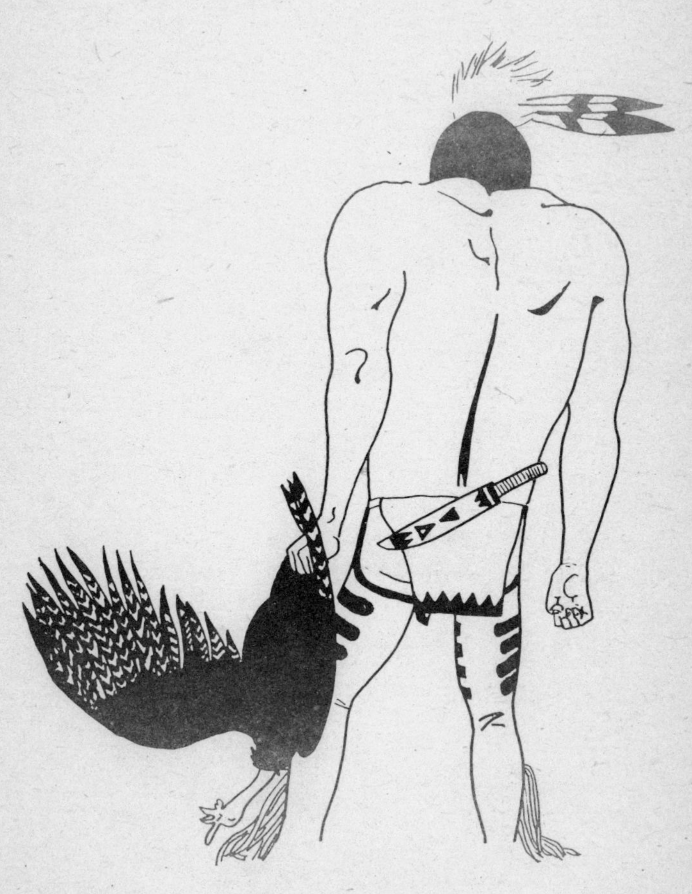

PUT TOGETHER A FEW WISE WORDS
IN FRONT OF THE ELDER ONES

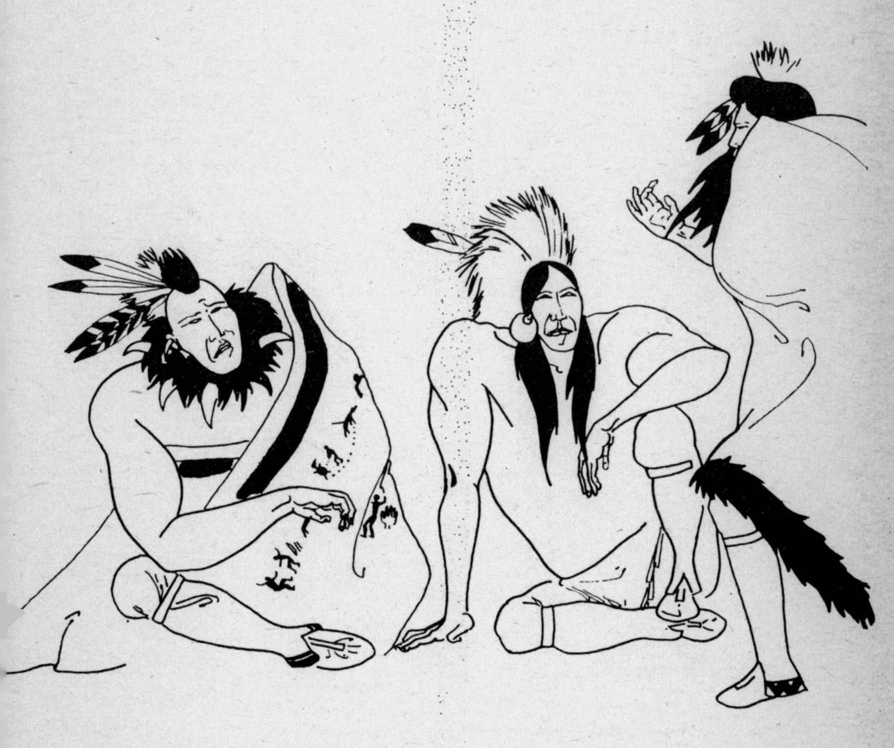

ALL BECAUSE SHE SMILED AT ME

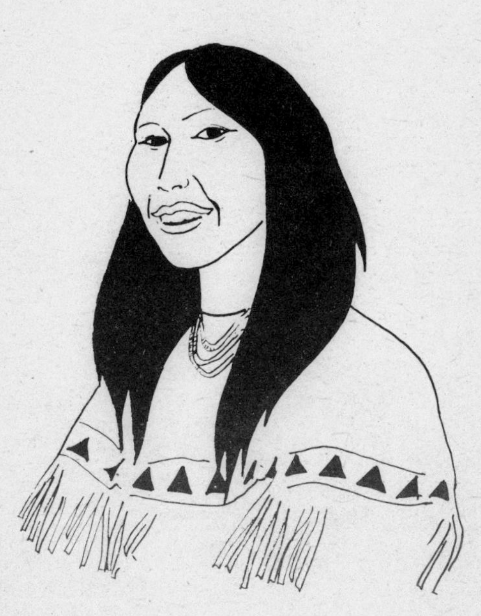

AND HER FATHER SAID
HE AIN'T GONNA GIVE HER
TO WHO'S NOT A MAN

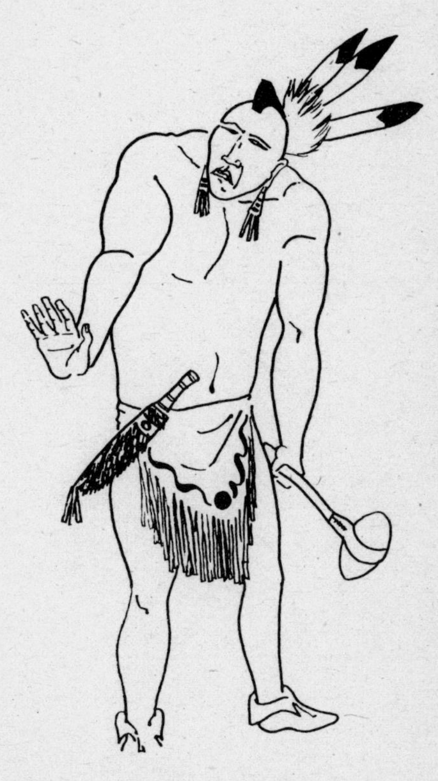

I HEARD THEM TALKING ABOUT HER
WITH LOVE IN THEIR MINDS
I HAVE SEEN THEM START THEIR DANCES
TO CALL HER OUT
GREAT NAMES I HEARD IN THE DARK OF THE NIGHT
BUT A NAME CAN'T STEAL THE BEAR'S CHILD
TO THE HOMELESS MAN
NOBODY SEWS HIS MOCASSINS
ALL HE HAD WAS A CEDAR FLUTE
WHO COULD GUESS THAT WITH THAT ONE
HE'D CALL HER
AND SHE'D RUN TO HIM?
NOW HE'S A BEAR
AND THE LITTLE BEARS OF SPRING
CALL HIM 'FATHER'

I HEARD THEM TALKING ABOUT HER
WITH LOVE IN THEIR MINDS

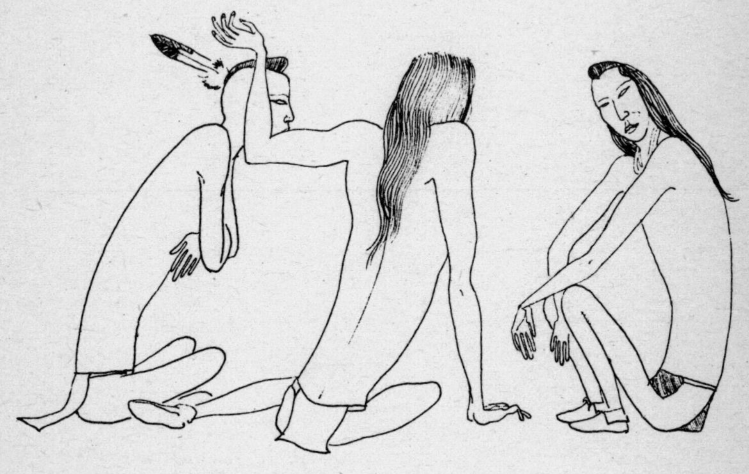

I HAVE SEEN THEM START THEIR DANCES
TO CALL HER OUT

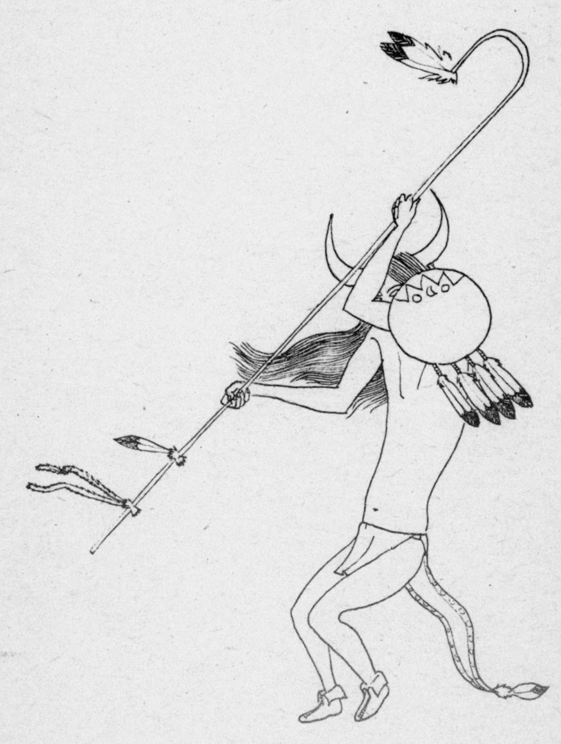

GREAT NAMES I HEARD IN THE DARK OF THE NIGHT

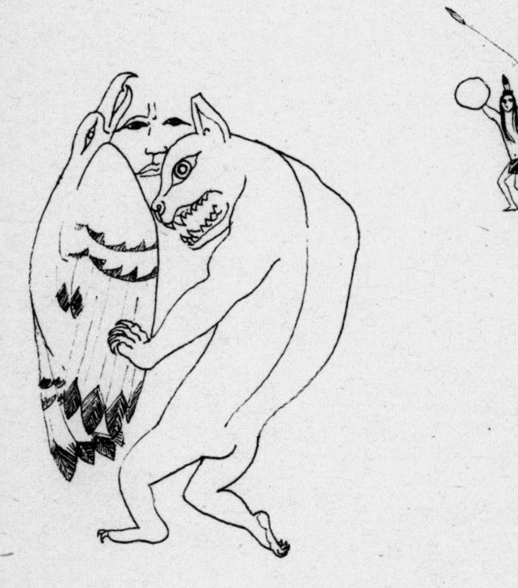

BUT A NAME CAN'T STEAL THE BEAR'S CHILD

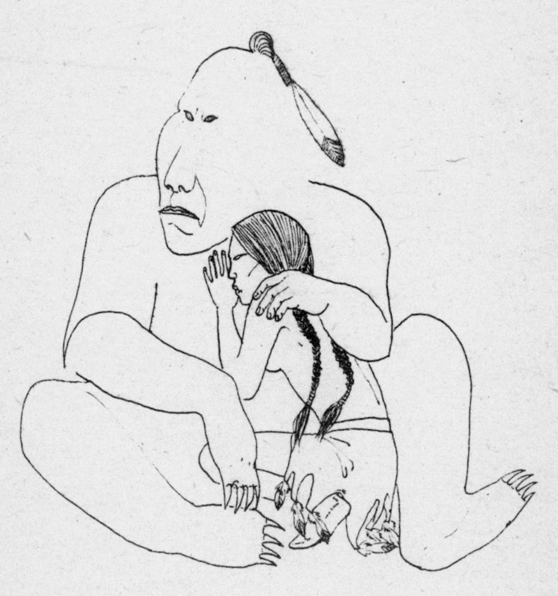

TO THE HOMELESS MAN
NOBODY SEWS HIS MOCASSINS
ALL HE HAD WAS A CEDAR FLUTE

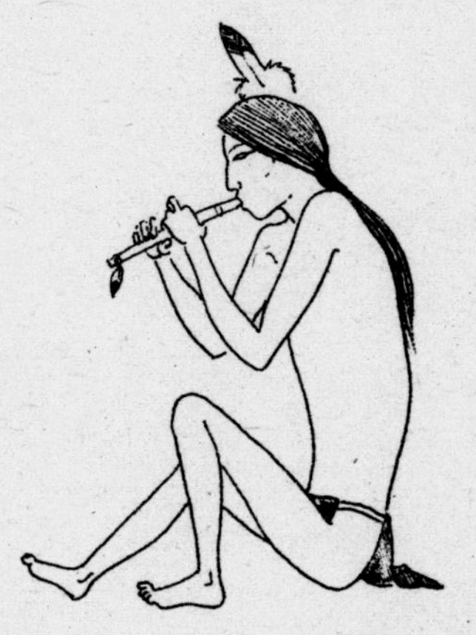

WHO COULD GUESS THAT WITH THAT ONE
HE'D CALL HER

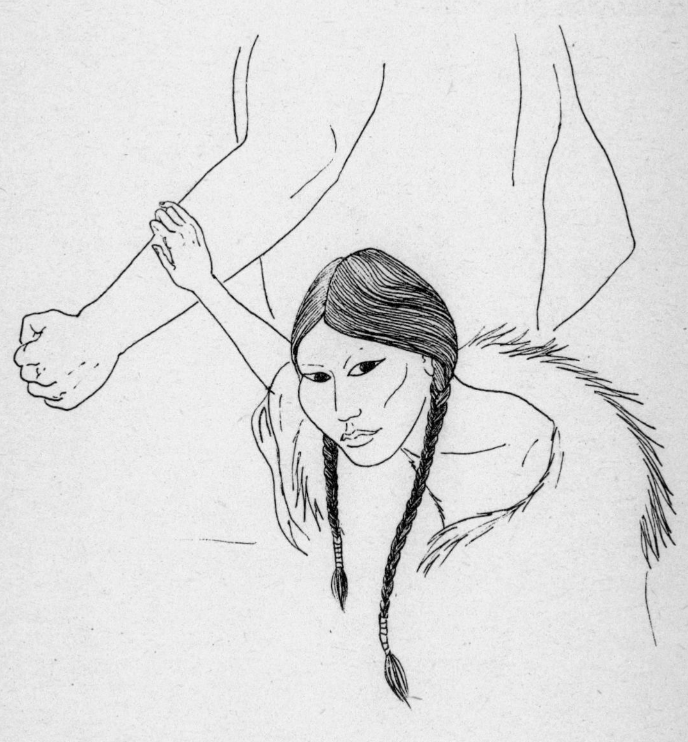

AND SHE'D RUN TO HIM?

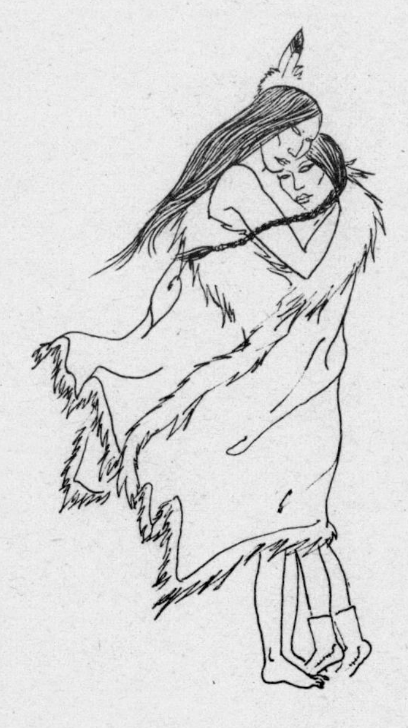

NOW HE'S A BEAR
AND THE LITTLE BEARS OF SPRING
CALL HIM 'FATHER'

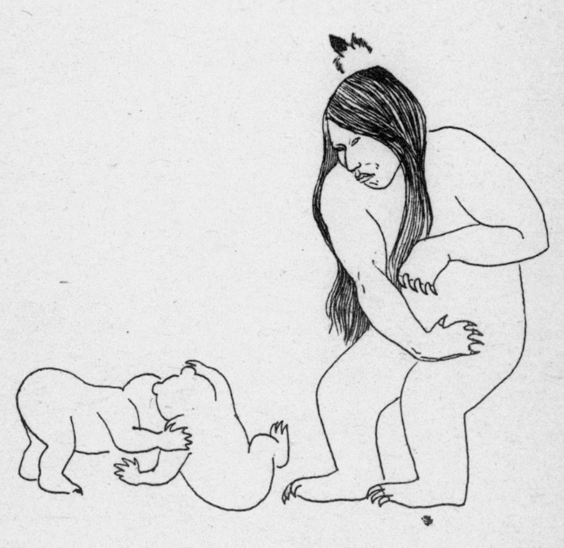

I HAD TO SEE HER HEART TO HAVE HER
   HAD TO SEE HIS HEART TO HAVE HIM
   WITH A SOUTH HORSE
   I CAME AT THE SCALP DANCE
   WITH TWO LITTLE BONES I LOST ALL I HAD
   AND STILL I WAS RICH
      THEN A COW
     RIGHT ON TOP OF THE HILL
AND IT WAS ALL OVER

I HAD TO SEE HER HEART TO HAVE HER

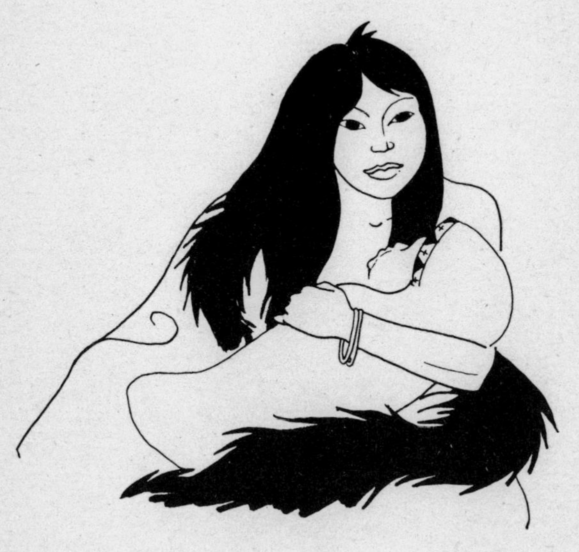

HAD TO SEE HIS HEART TO HAVE HIM

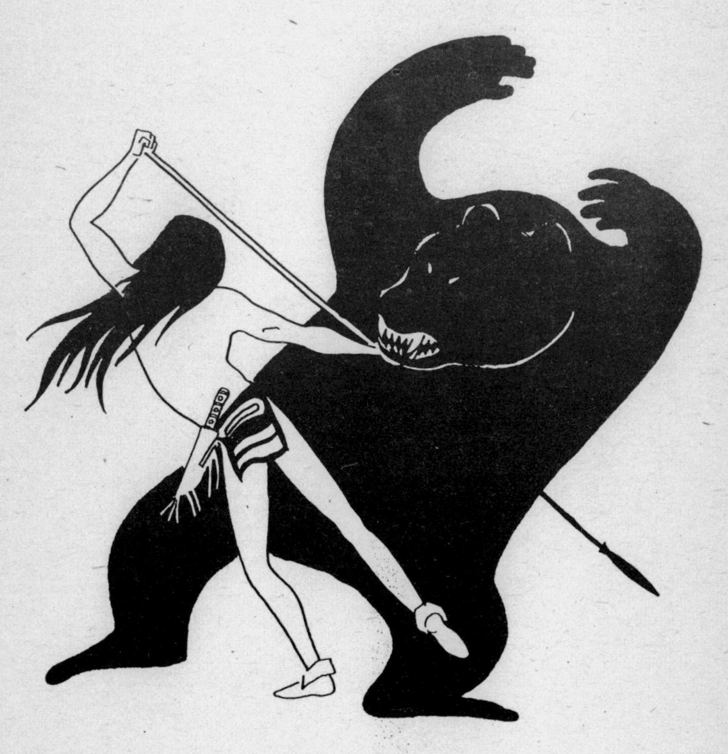

WITH A SOUTH HORSE

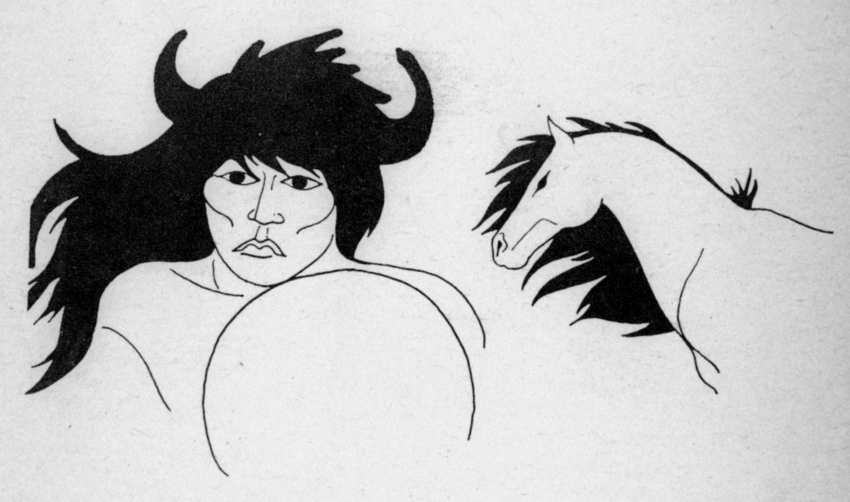

I CAME AT THE SCALP DANCE

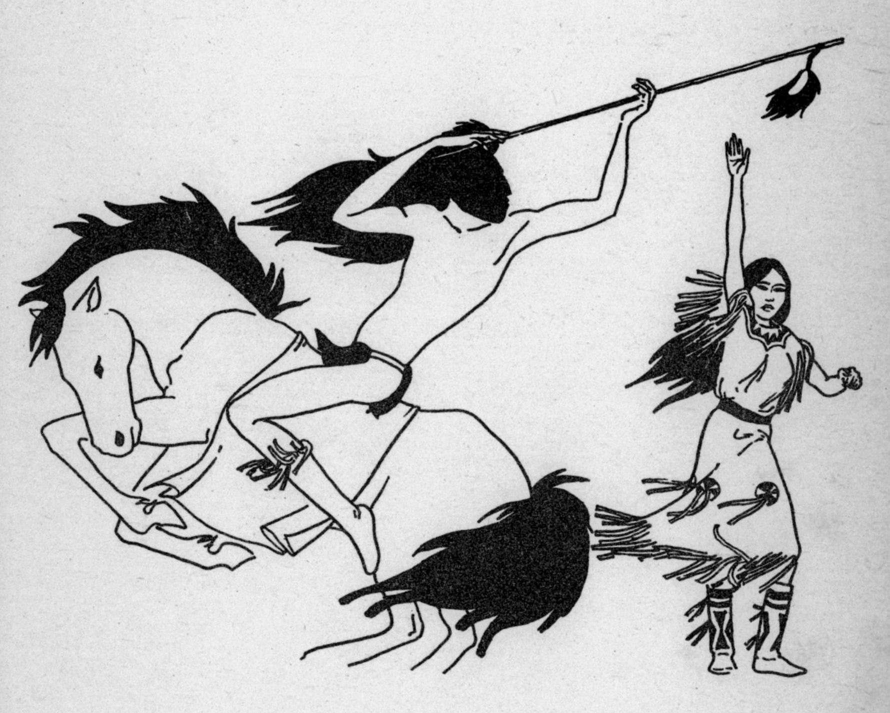

WITH TWO LITTLE BONES I LOST ALL I HAD

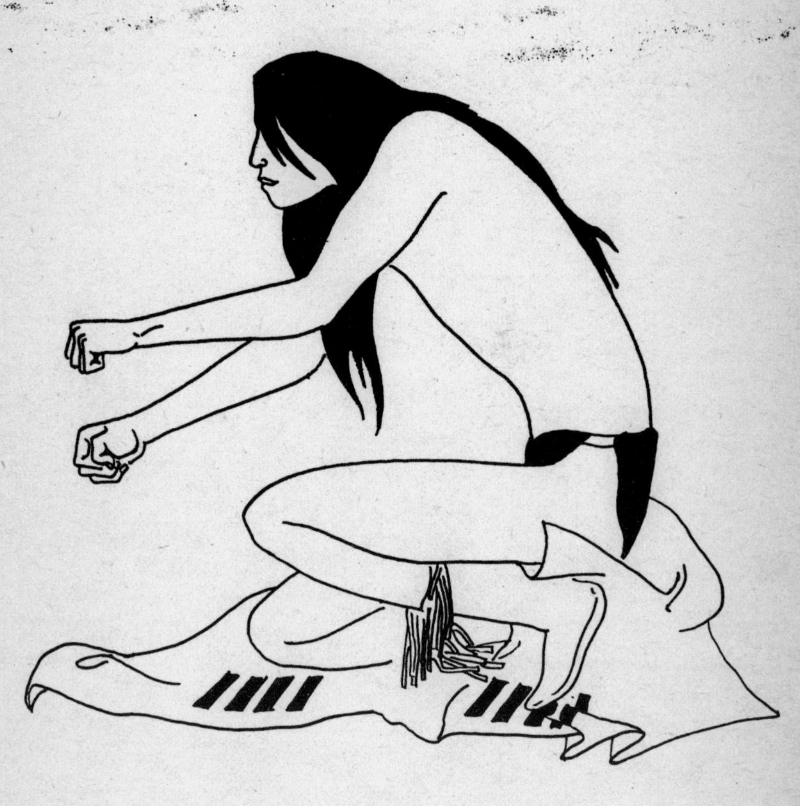

AND STILL I WAS RICH

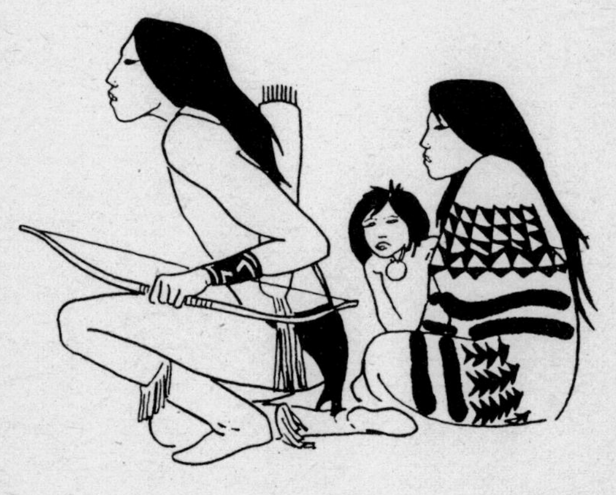

THEN A COW
RIGHT ON TOP OF THE HILL

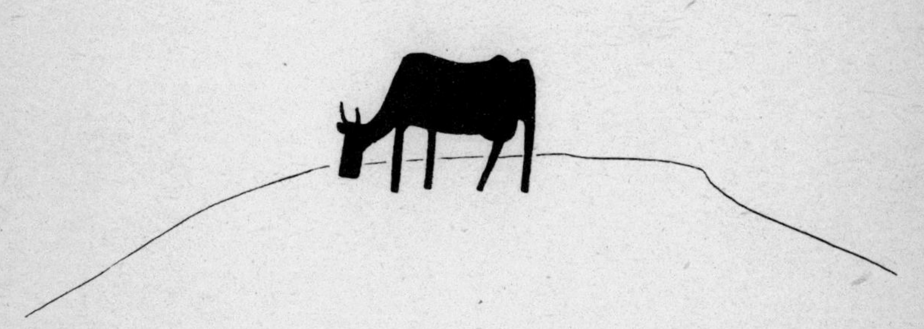

AND IT WAS ALL OVER

SEVEN MEN ON THE ROCK UPON THE HOUSE
THE DEADMAN'S HEAD IS LAUGHING
AT MY MISTAKES
A LAZY FLYIN' OF CROWS IN THE SKY
BRINGS ME AWAY
IN A RETURNLESS RUN
LIKE RED LEAVES
CARRIED BY THE AUTUMN WIND
WITH AN IRON BLADE
I WAS TRYING TO WRITE ON ROCK HEARTS
HOPING TO SEE THEM LAUGH
HOPING TO SEE THEM CRY

SEVEN MEN ON THE ROCK UPON THE HOUSE

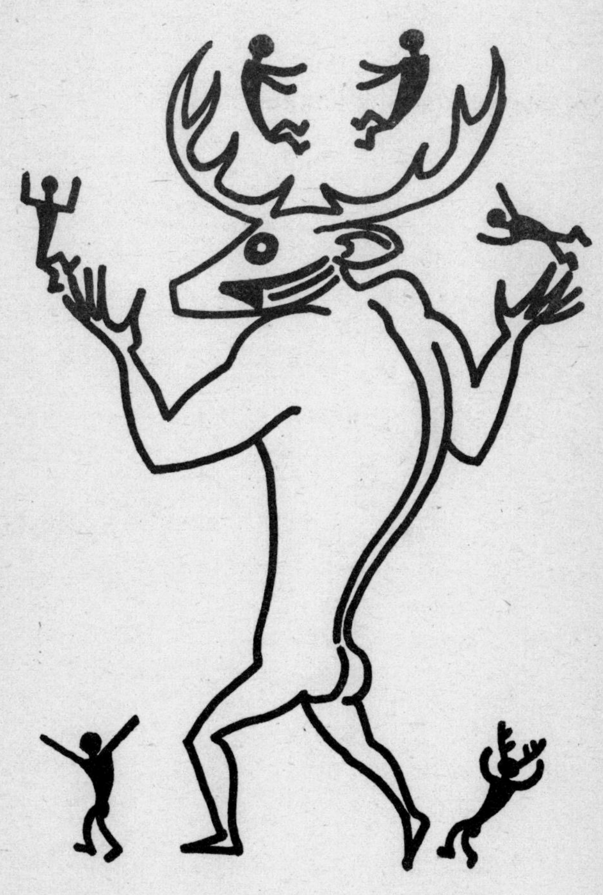

THE DEADMAN'S HEAD IS LAUGHING
AT MY MISTAKES

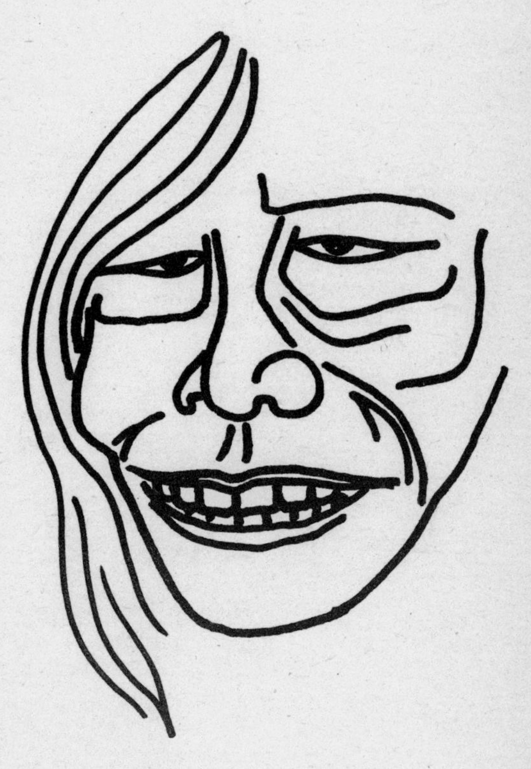

A LAZY FLYIN' OF CROWS IN THE SKY

BRINGS ME AWAY
IN A RETURNLESS RUN

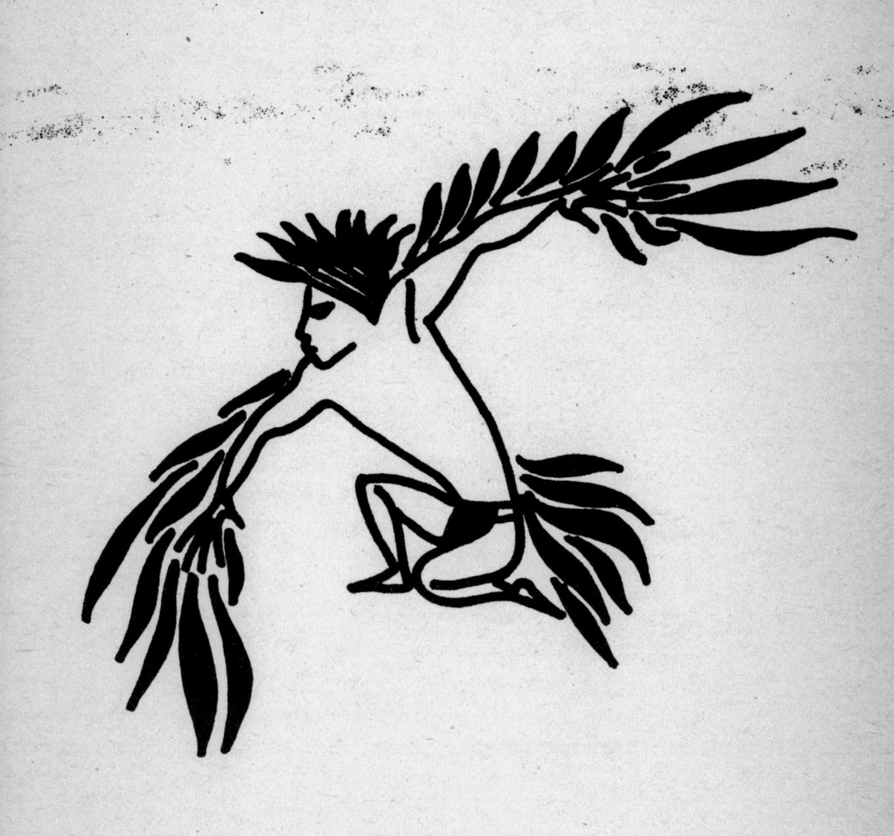

LIKE RED LEAVES
CARRIED BY THE AUTUMN WIND

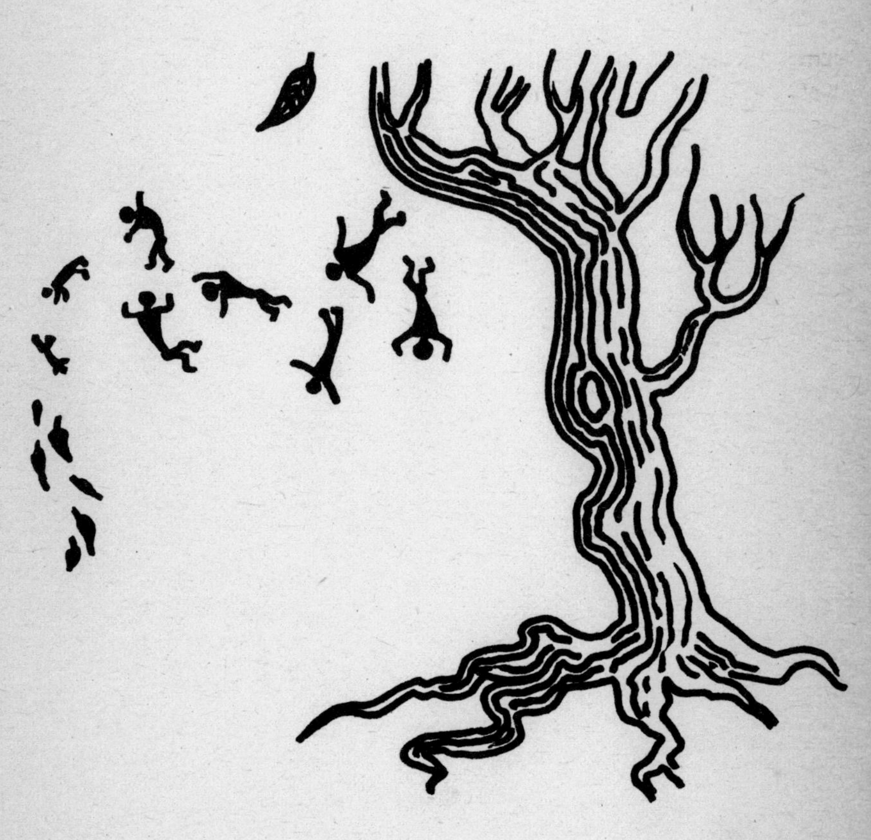

WITH AN IRON BLADE
I WAS TRYING TO WRITE ON ROCK HEARTS

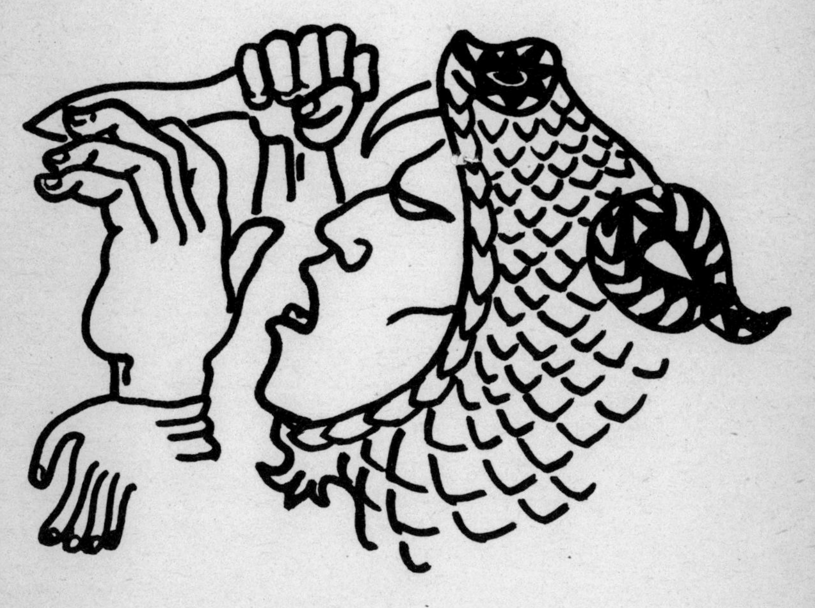

HOPING TO SEE THEM LAUGH

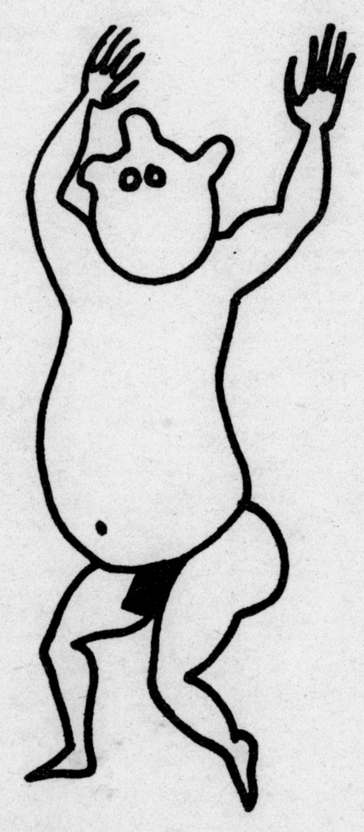

HOPING TO SEE THEM CRY

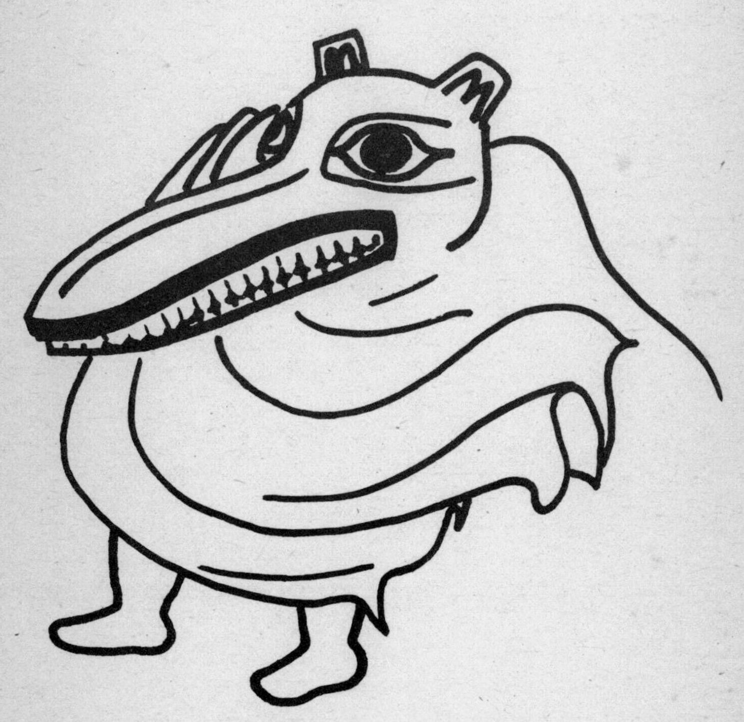

I WAS MIXING STARS AND SAND
IN FRONT OF HIM
BUT HE COULDN'T UNDERSTAND
I WAS KEEPING THE LIGHTNING OF
THE THUNDER IN MY PURSE
JUST IN FRONT OF HIM
BUT HE COULDN'T UNDERSTAND
AND I HAD BEEN KILLED A THOUSAND TIMES
RIGHT AT HIS FEET
BUT HE HADN'T UNDERSTOOD

I WAS MIXING STARS AND SAND

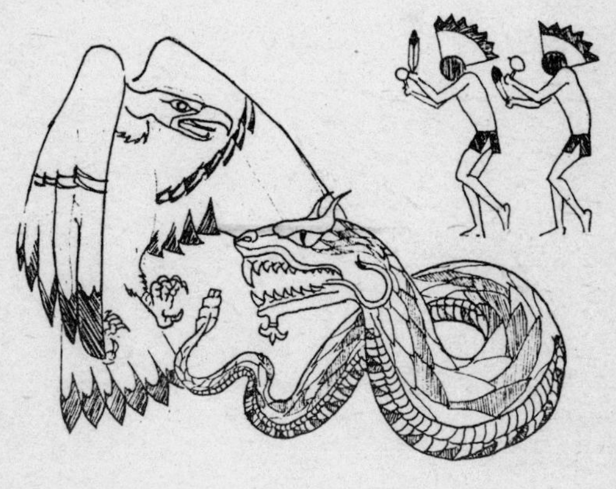

IN FRONT OF HIM

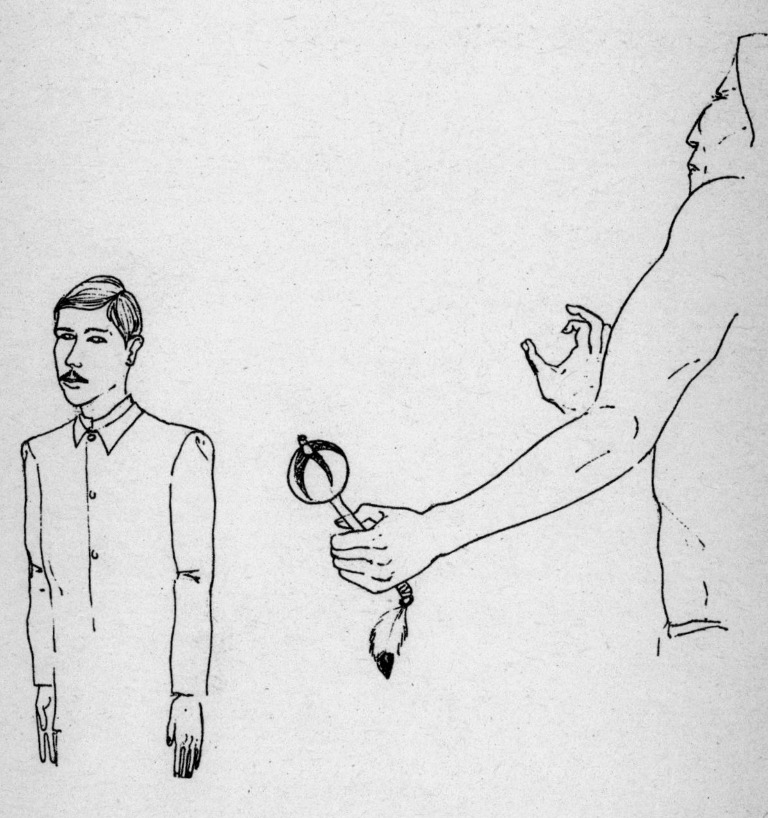

BUT HE COULDN'T UNDERSTAND

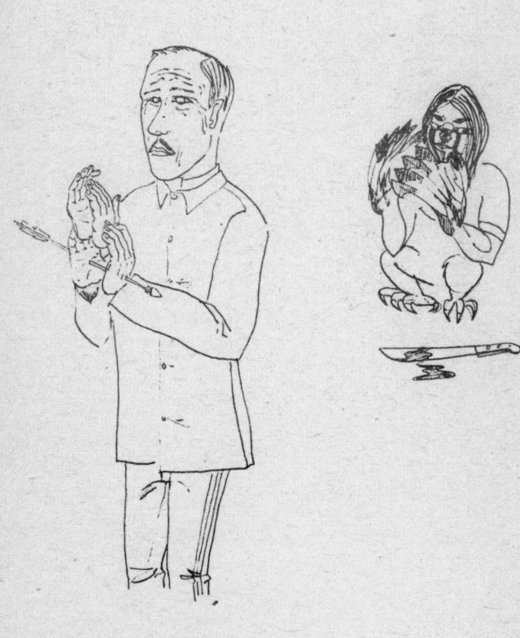

I WAS KEEPING THE LIGHTNING
THE THUNDER IN MY PURSE

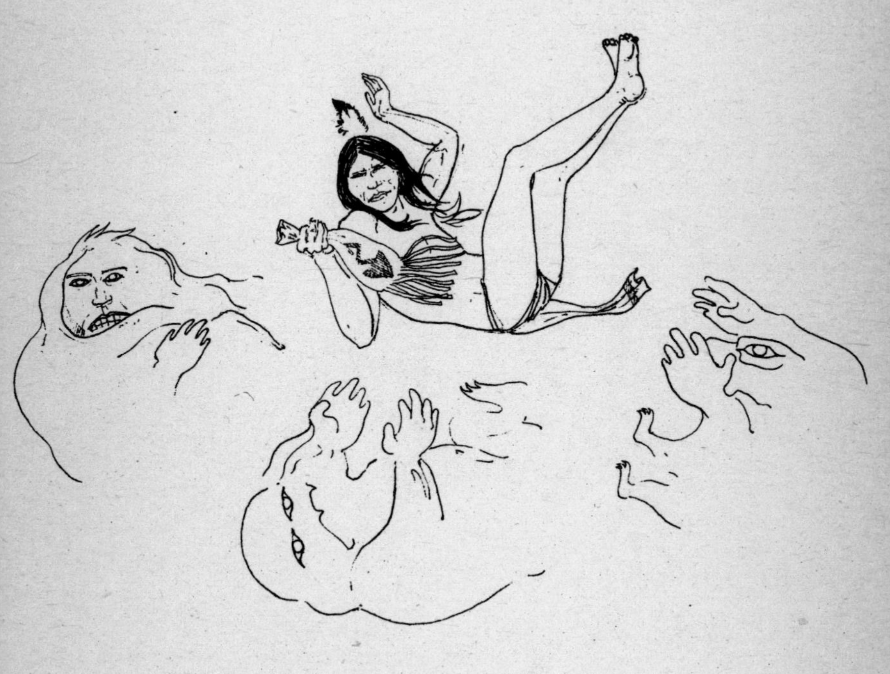

JUST IN FRONT OF HIM

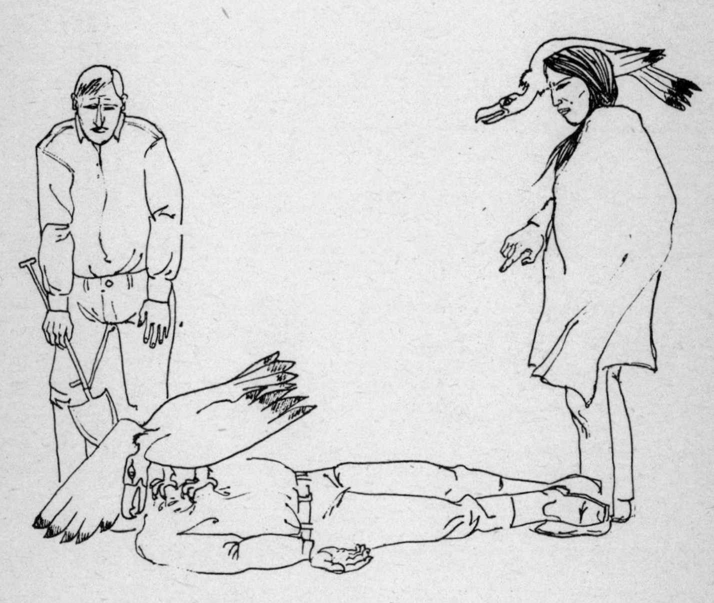

BUT HE COULDN'T UNDERSTAND

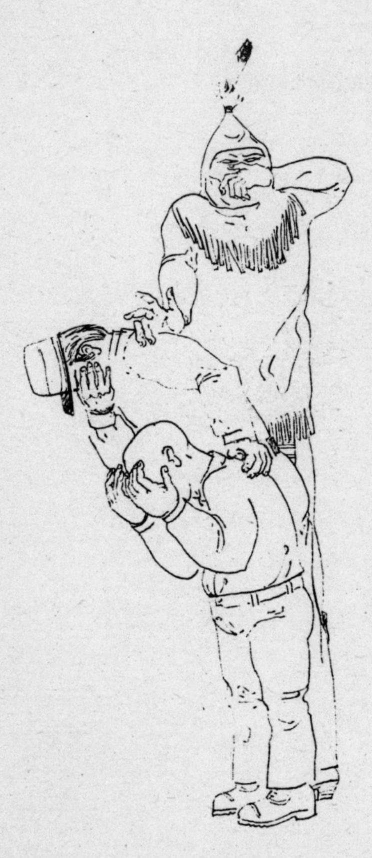

AND I HAD BEEN KILLED A THOUSAND TIMES
RIGHT AT HIS FEET

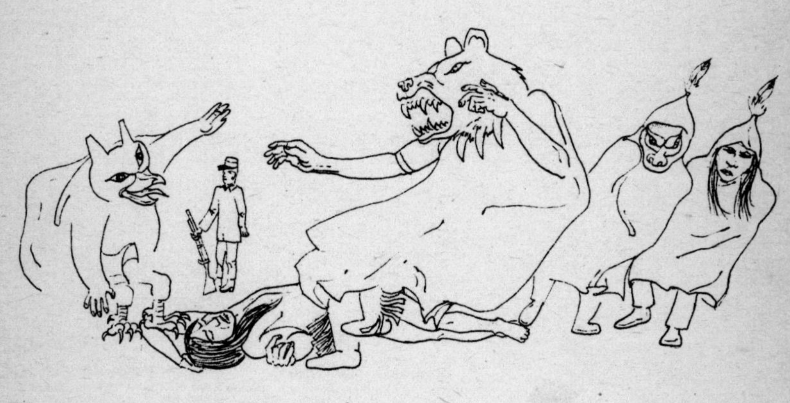

BUT HE HADN'T UNDERSTOOD

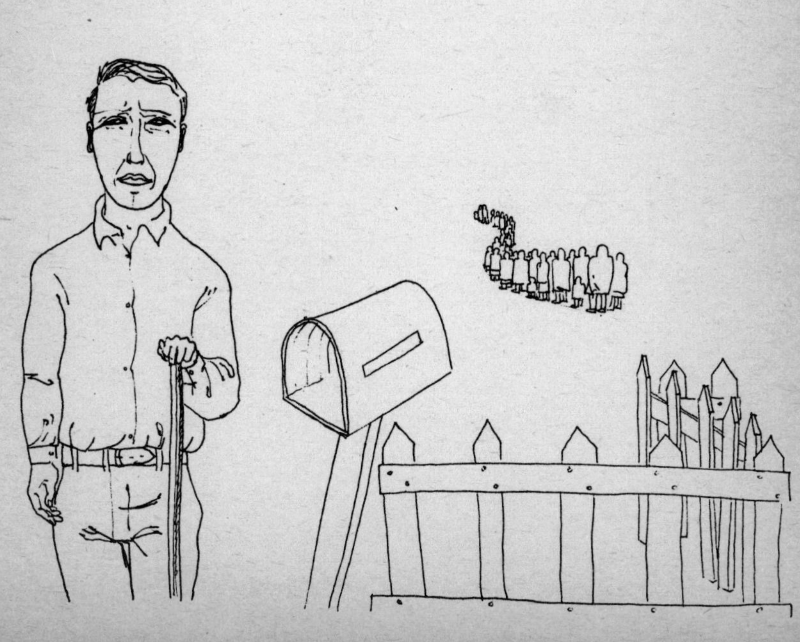

LITTLE TRACES IN MY MIND
BROUGHT ME BACK WHERE I WAS BORN
AND THERE WASN'T ANY EXPLANATION
JUST MY BACK SHOOK
AT THE CRYING OF MY DYING MOTHER

LITTLE TRACES IN MY MIND

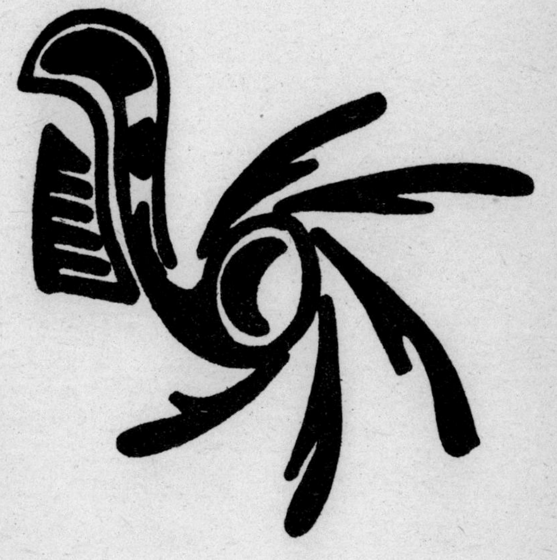

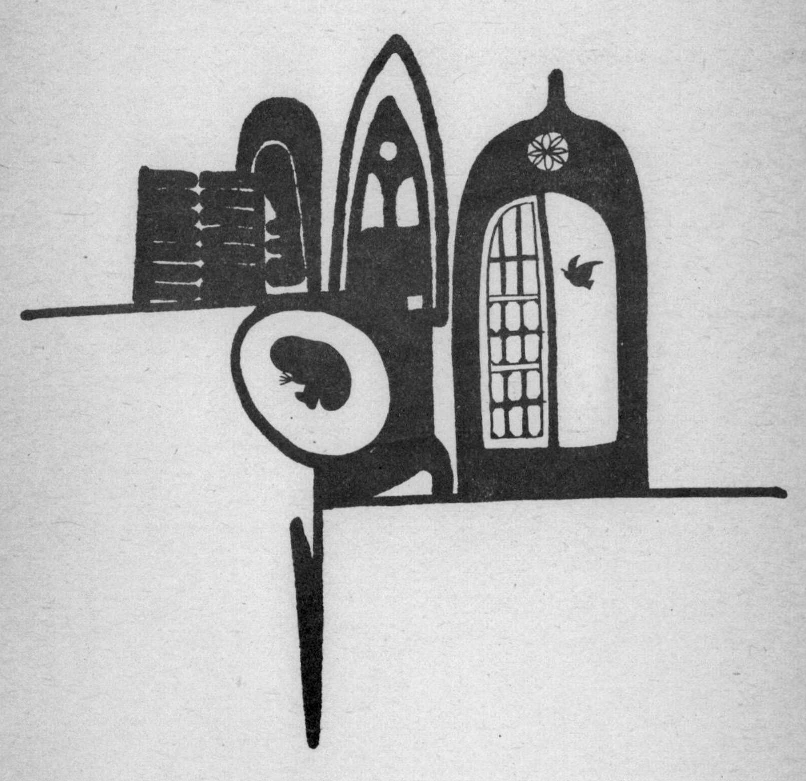

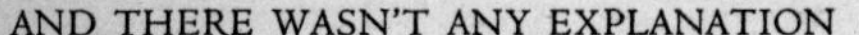

AND THERE WASN'T ANY EXPLANATION

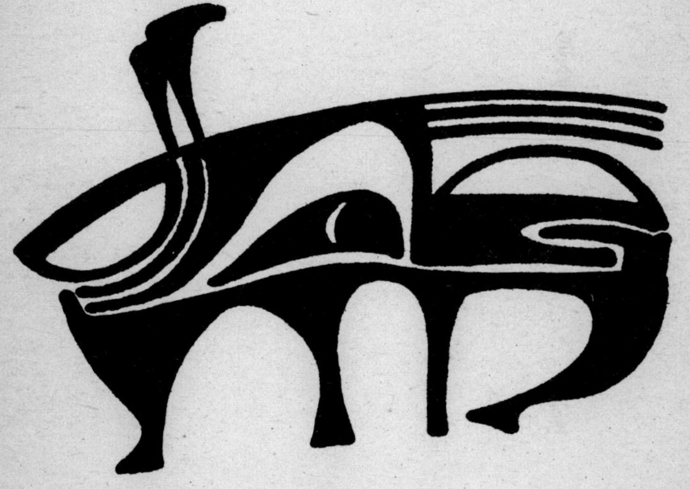

JUST MY BACK SHOOK

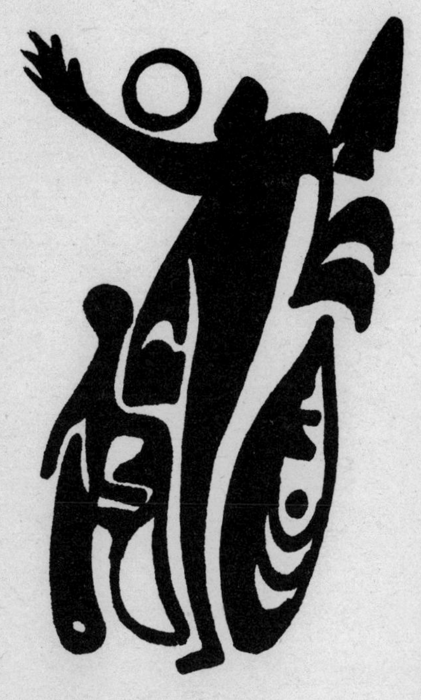

AT THE CRYING OF MY DYING MOTHER

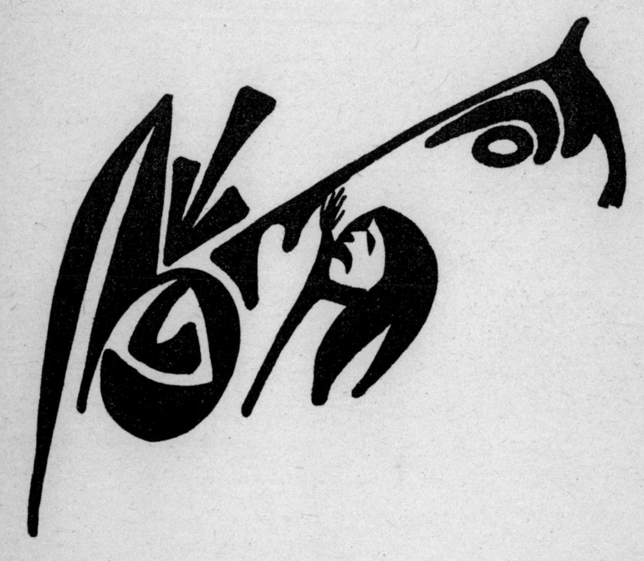